KERSTIN LOKRANTZ

CROSS-STITCH ON CLOTHES

Translated from the Swedish by
Päivi Crofts

PENGUIN BOOKS

Penguin Books Ltd, Harmondsworth, Middlesex, England
Penguin Books, 625 Madison Avenue, New York, New York 10022, U.S.A.
Penguin Books Australia Ltd, Ringwood, Victoria, Australia
Penguin Books Canada Ltd, 2801 John Street, Markham, Ontario, Canada L3R 1B4
Penguin Books (N.Z.) Ltd, 182–190 Wairau Road, Auckland 10, New Zealand

First published under the title *Kors Stygn på Kläder* by Bokförlaget Prisma
Stockholm, 1977
This translation published in Penguin Books 1979

Pictures on pp. 3, 4 and 5 from the Nordiska Museet
Photographs by Nisse Pettersson
Layout by Lena Anderson

Copyright © Kerstin Lokrantz, 1977
English translation © Penguin Books, 1979
All rights reserved

Made and printed in Great Britain by
Fletcher & Son Ltd, Norwich
Set in Monophoto Ehrhardt

Except in the United States of America, this book is
sold subject to the condition that it shall not, by
way of trade or otherwise, be lent, re-sold, hired out,
or otherwise circulated without the publisher's prior
consent in any form of binding or cover other than
that in which it is published and without a similar
condition including this condition being imposed on
the subsequent purchaser

Cross-stitch embroidery is an enjoyable art which anyone can learn. Many of the patterns shown in this book were sewn by children.

The equipment is simple: needles, cotton embroidery thread, which comes in many beautiful colours, and rug or tapestry canvas which is sold in most haberdashery and needlework shops. The canvas is used as a grid to guide the size of the stitches on plain fabrics. Another method is to use checked fabric and sew your pattern straight on to the material, using the squares as a grid.

Old textiles with cross-stitch decoration and cross-stitch samplers can be seen in many museums. Like folk music, the designs have a rich tradition. The same motifs appear time and time again, with small variations, in old pattern books.

I have managed to collect a lot of fine old patterns, for many examples of cross-stitch embroidery, designed and sewn by skilful workers, have been preserved. They came from museums and also from friends, who lent me embroidery worked by their mothers and grandmothers.

In the past, sheets, handkerchiefs and underwear were embroidered with cross-stitch. It seems a pity, though, that such lovely embroidery should be hidden under clothes, or in linen cupboards or bottom drawers. The aim of this book is to inspire you to decorate everyday clothes, jackets and jeans, and party dresses too, with cross-stitch. 'Nothing is so beautiful that it can't be cross-stitched,' proclaims an old book proudly.

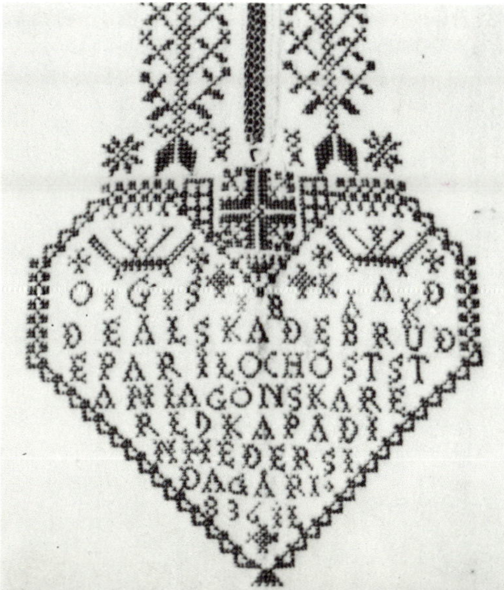

Bridal shirts from the beginning of the nineteenth century. These shirts were made by ordinary people. A bride would make a shirt and embroider it in fine cross-stitch with the name, and the year of her marriage; the groom would be given this shirt as a present on their wedding day.

Shirts were made of hand-woven linen or cotton and the embroidery was usually red. It was done on the straight grain of the fabric with tiny cross-stitches. These garments were usually worn on only two occasions: as a wedding shirt and as a shroud.

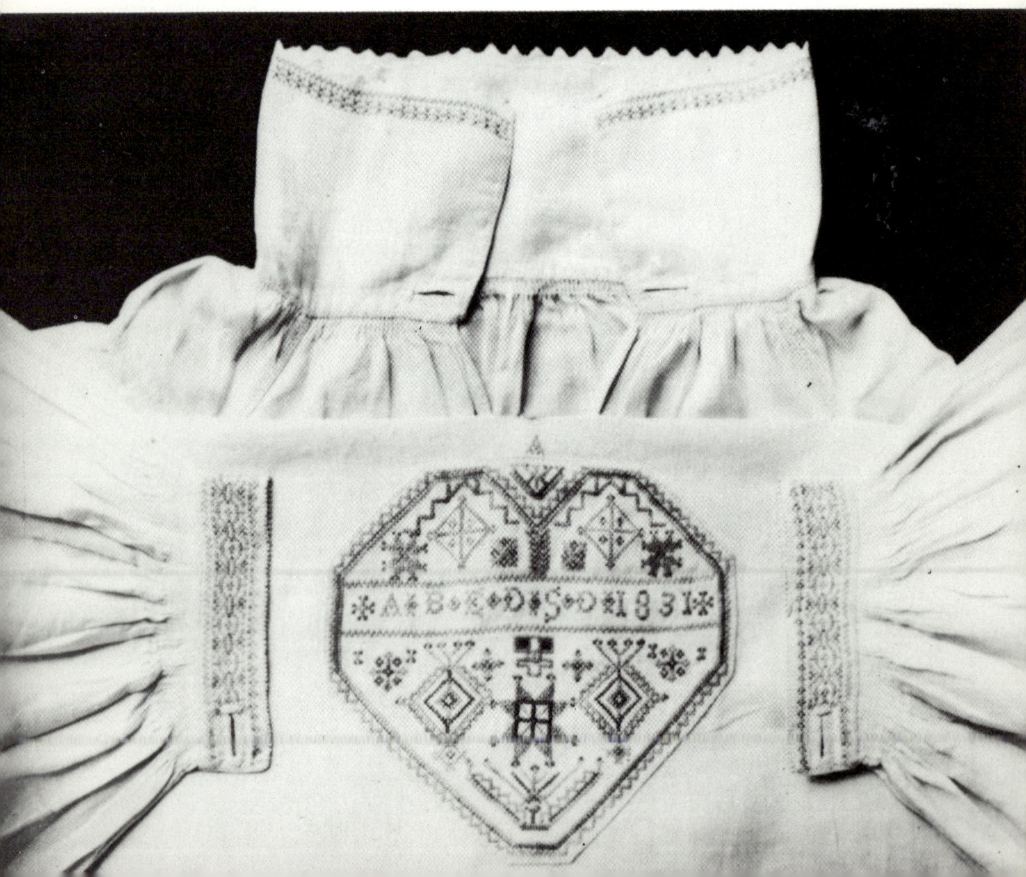

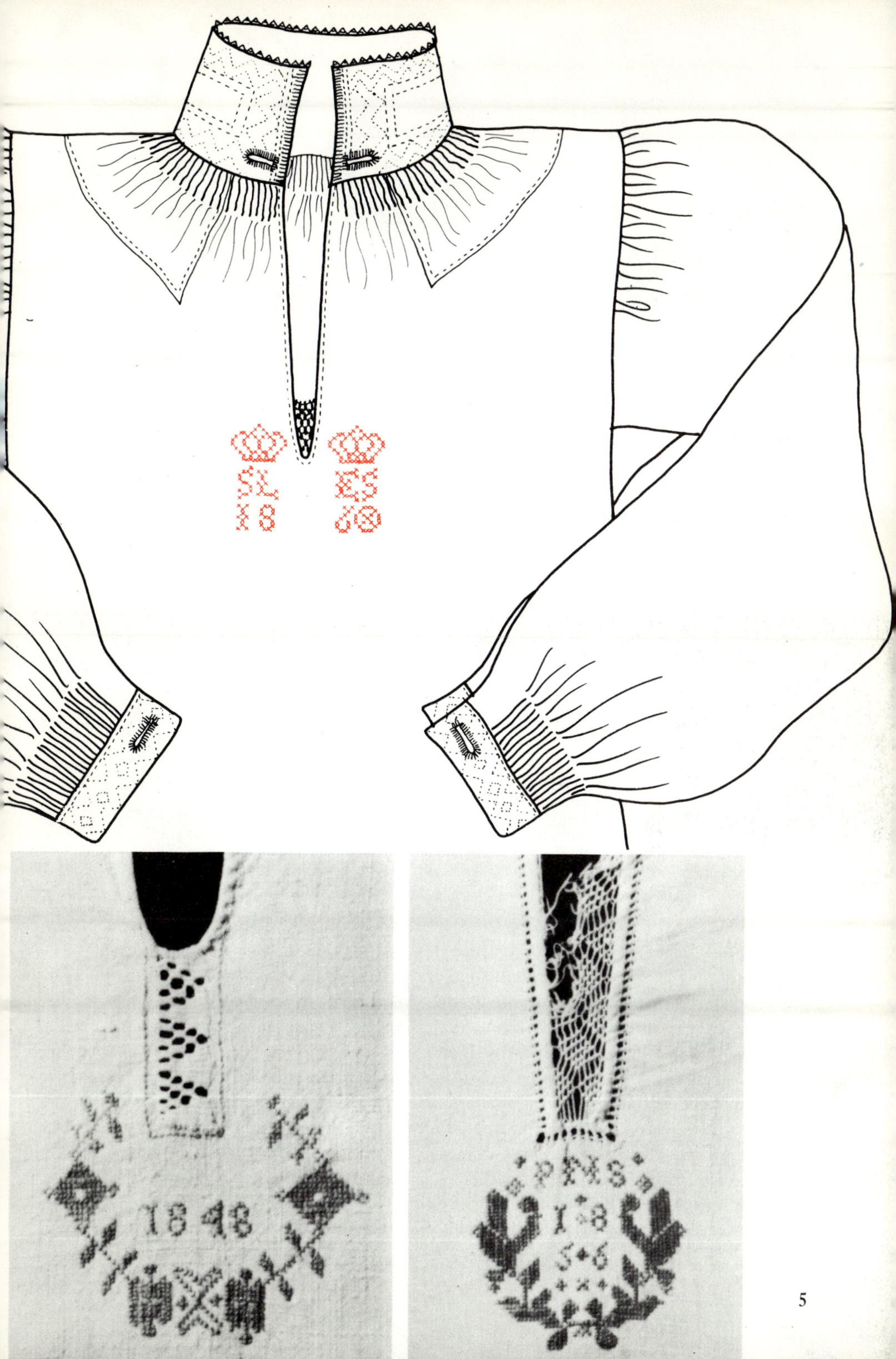
SL
18
ES
1848
PMS

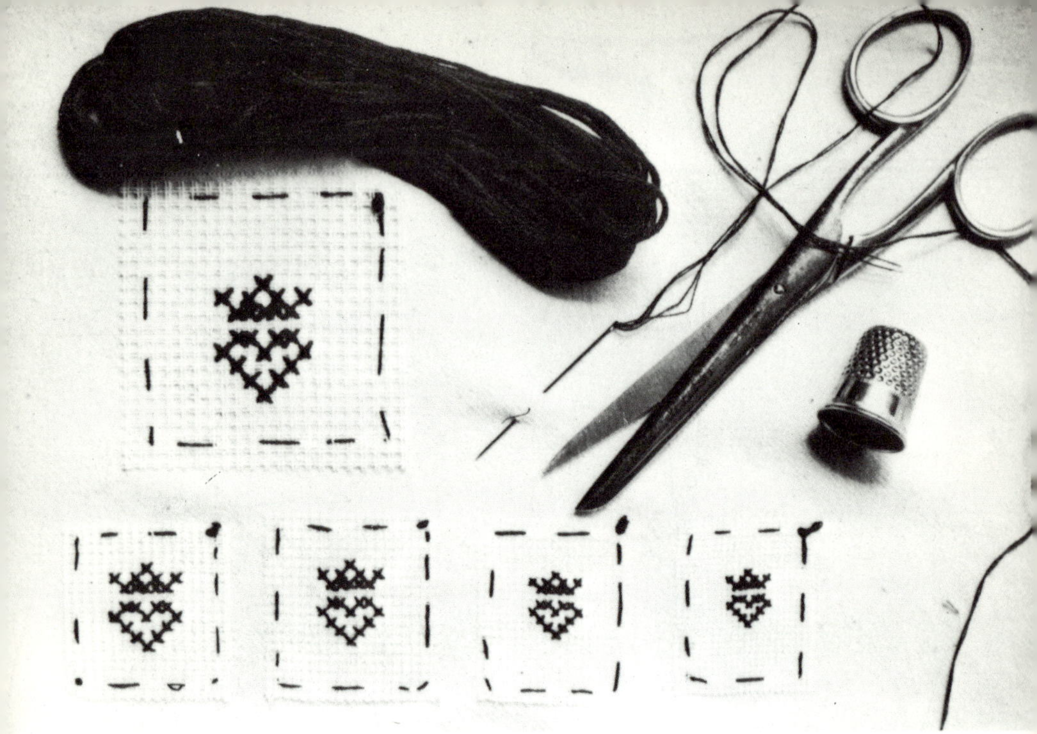

Here you can see how the size of the design varies according to the coarseness of the canvas.

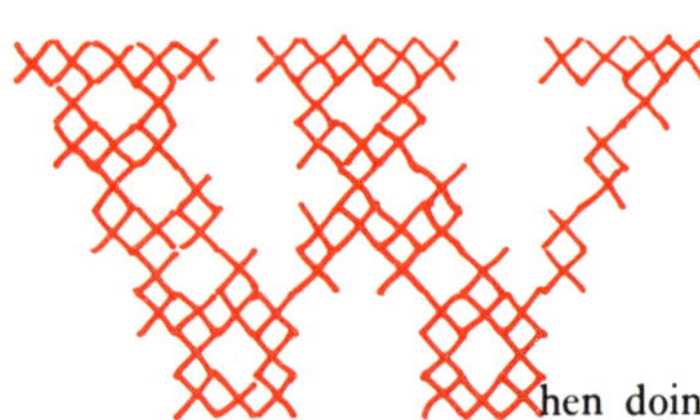

hen doing cross-stitch, make sure that you have good tools: needles of different sizes, a thimble, a pair of small scissors and cotton embroidery thread or crochet thread. Canvas comes in various grades and can be bought by the metre. Coarse canvas produces a large pattern; a fine canvas a smaller one. Embroidery thread can be divided into several strands: use two except when sewing on a thick material, such as towelling. When choosing a pattern from the book, look at it with your eyes screwed up to get an idea of how it will look eventually. Remember that the design will be much smaller when it is sewn.

Before you start to sew, count the number of squares in the height and width of the design. Then count the same number of squares on the canvas. This gives you the size of the motif. Cut out a piece of canvas a little larger than the pattern and tack it to the fabric where you want the embroidery to be. The grain of the canvas should lie in the same direction as the grain of the fabric.

The cross-stitching is worked by sewing through the canvas and fabric together – the

A motif sewn on canvas and fabric.

Unravel the canvas, thread by thread.

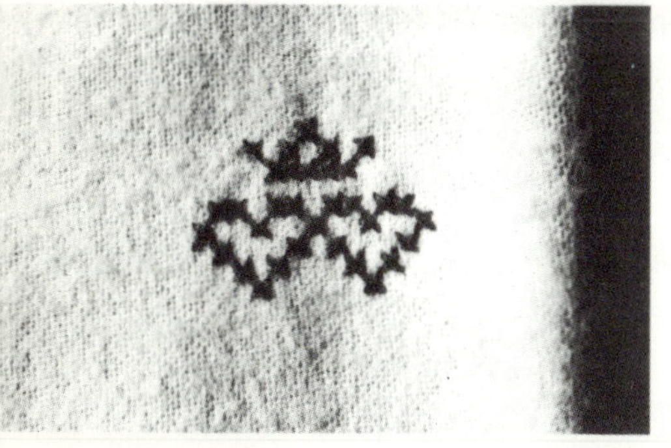

A finished pattern. Press from the wrong side of the fabric.

canvas is merely a guide and is later removed.

To get the best results, always sew first from bottom left to top right, and then from bottom right to top left. You can also sew a whole row of half crosses, beginning at the left and coming back from the right. The needle should go in from the top. Always fasten off the thread at the back on the under-side of the stitching, never on the right side.

When the pattern is finished unpick the tacking and unravel the canvas threads; then ease them out carefully, one by one.

Put the needle in through the middle of the canvas square. Don't sew into the canvas threads as they will eventually have to be pulled out.

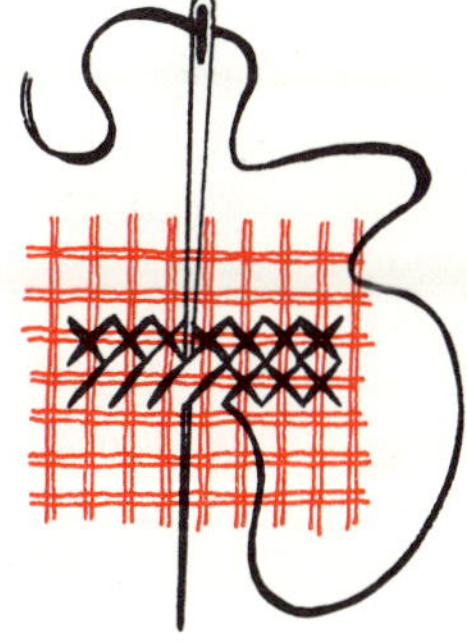

A wreath in several shades of blue, embroidered on a sun top. Patterns for the alphabet are given at the end of the book.

Birds on striped cloth. This pattern is taken from an old source.
Below: Birds and a heart sewn on denim in red, blue and white.

JP

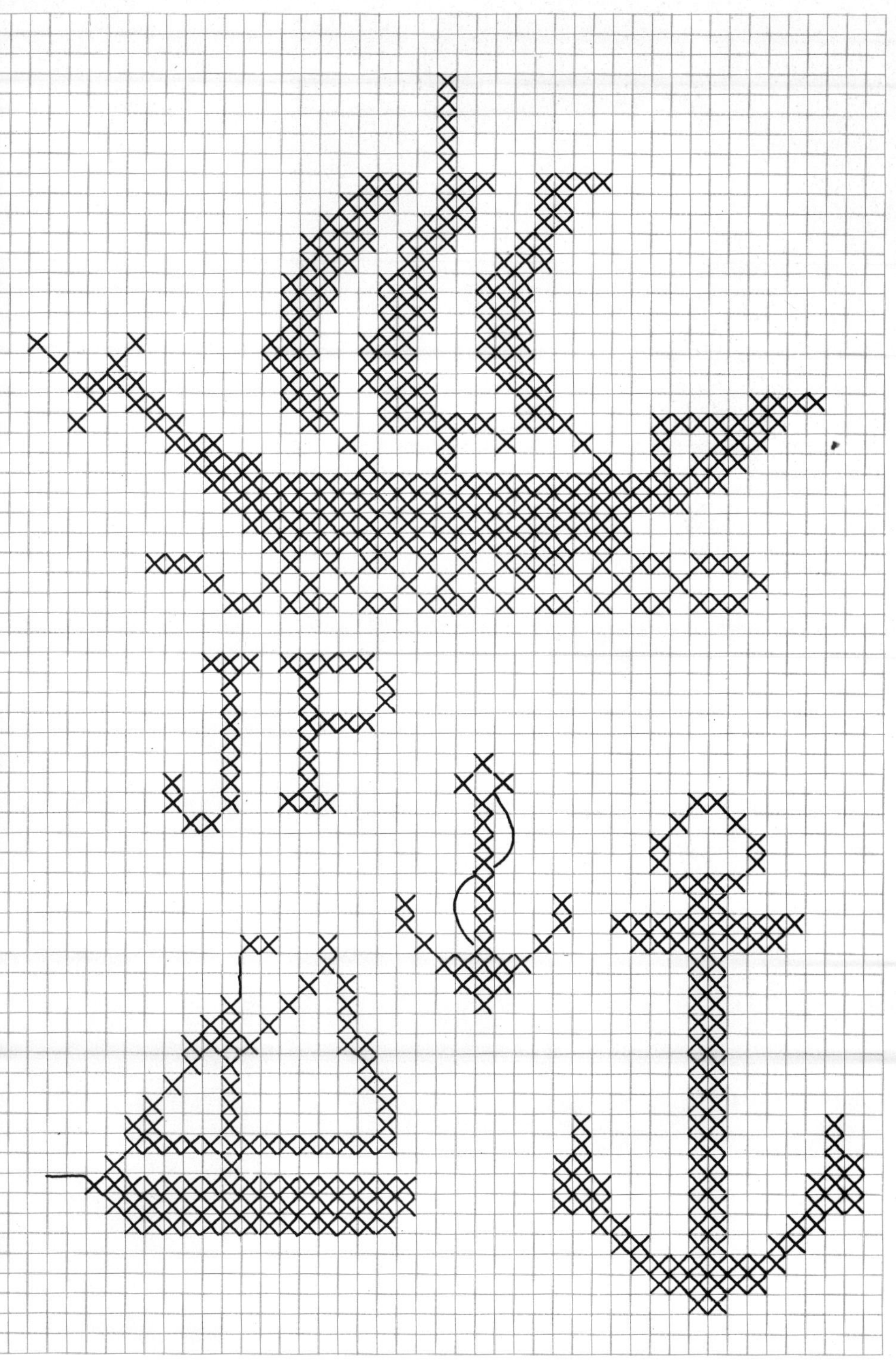

On the scarf canvas has been used to guide the stitches. On the apron the motif is worked directly on the fabric following the squares.

↑ *centre*

(*The other half of the pattern is shown on p. 89.*)

A splendid crown embroidered in pink and pale blue on an old coat. Crowns can be combined with letters or names.

Name surrounded by a wreath on a sailcloth bag. Cycling jacket with three cyclists in a row.

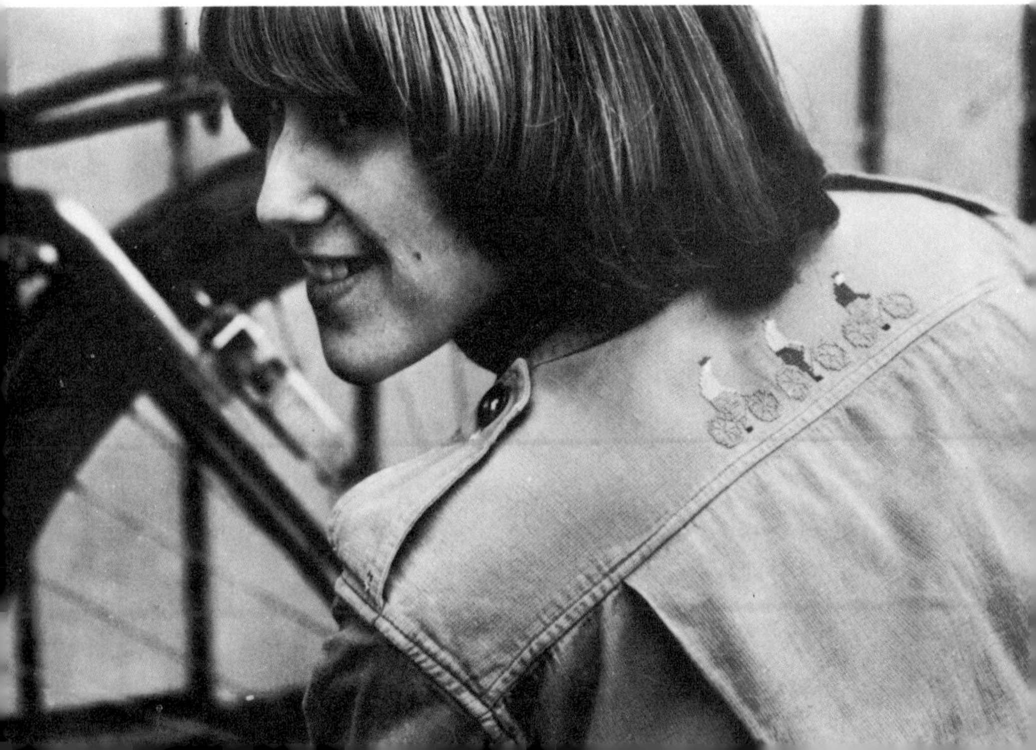

IP

IP

Children's clothes with borders sewn directly on the material. Use three strands of embroidery cotton or crochet thread.

HÖGALIDS RADIO
Just idag!
RING 63 06 60
CHOCK-PRISER

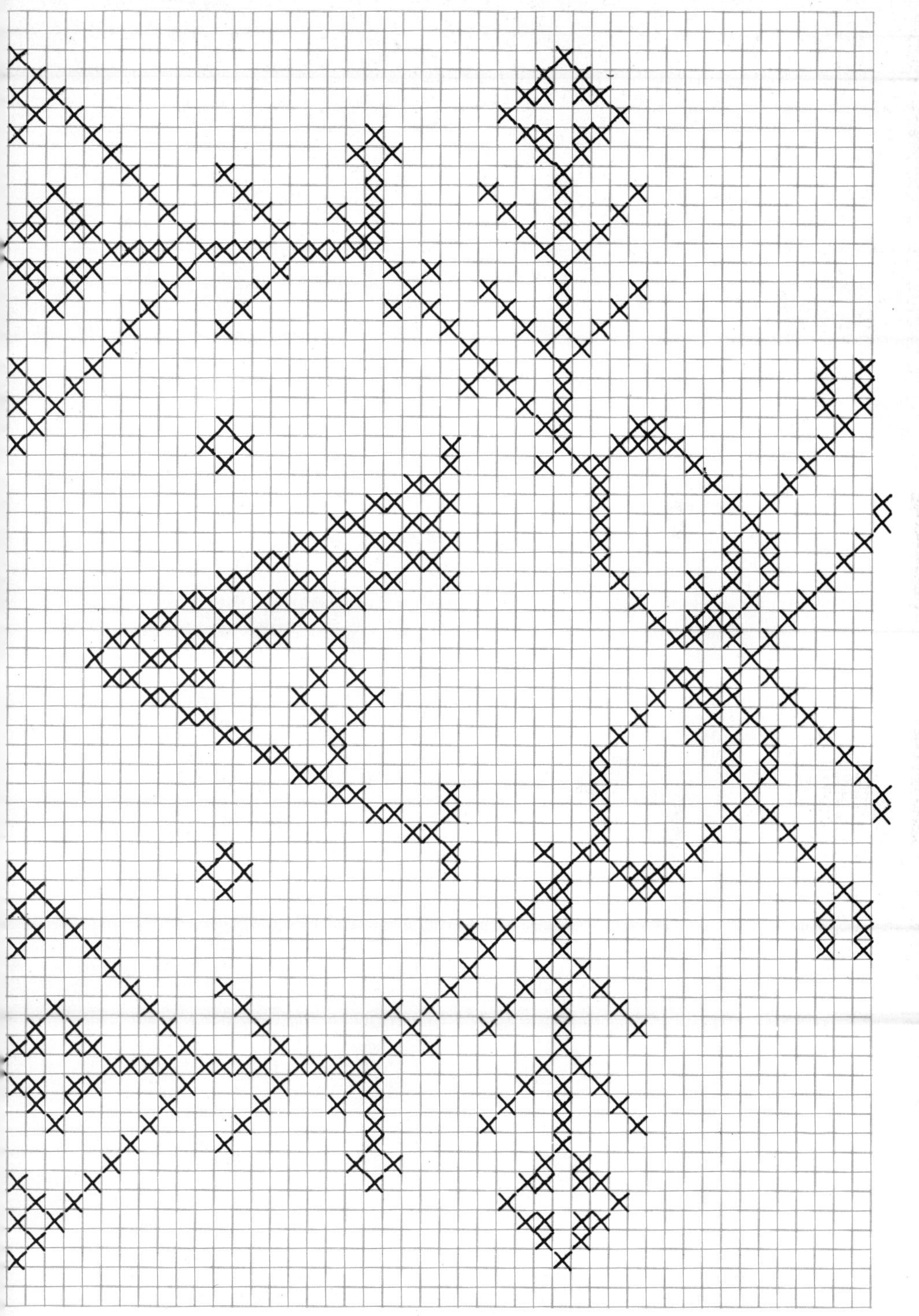

A dress with a little flower on the front to hide a stain which would not come off in the wash. The flower is done in the same colours as the borders.

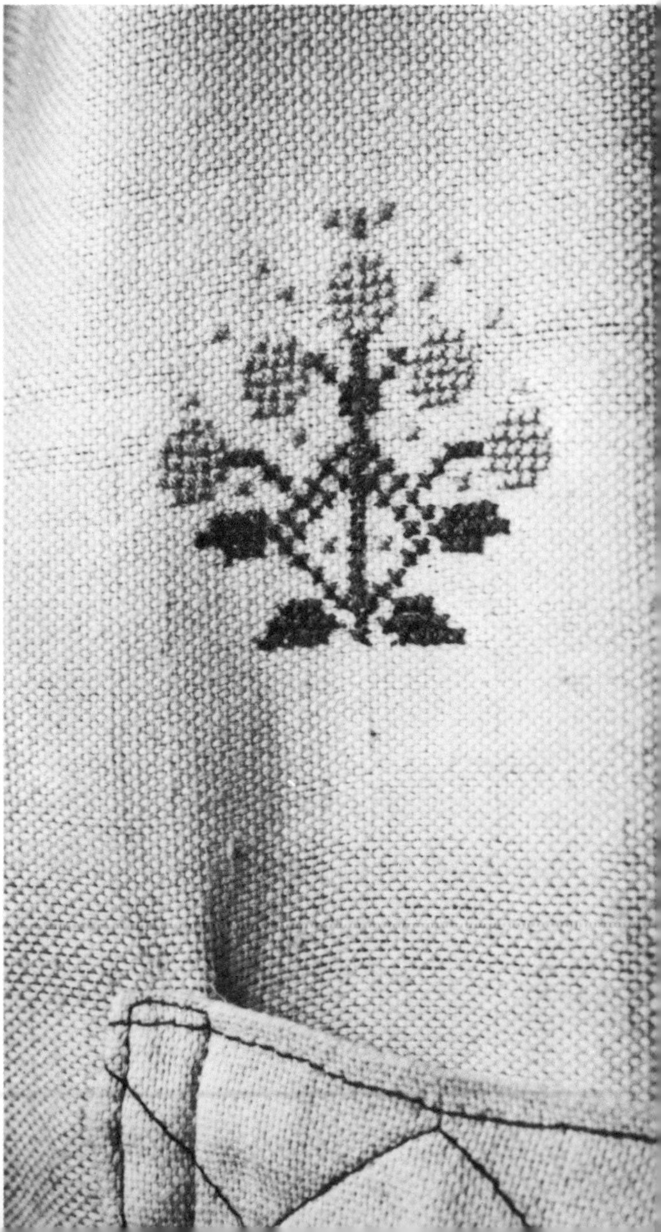

Cross-stitch on a black background. For the patterns on the dress on the right see pp. 11, 17, 27 and 43.

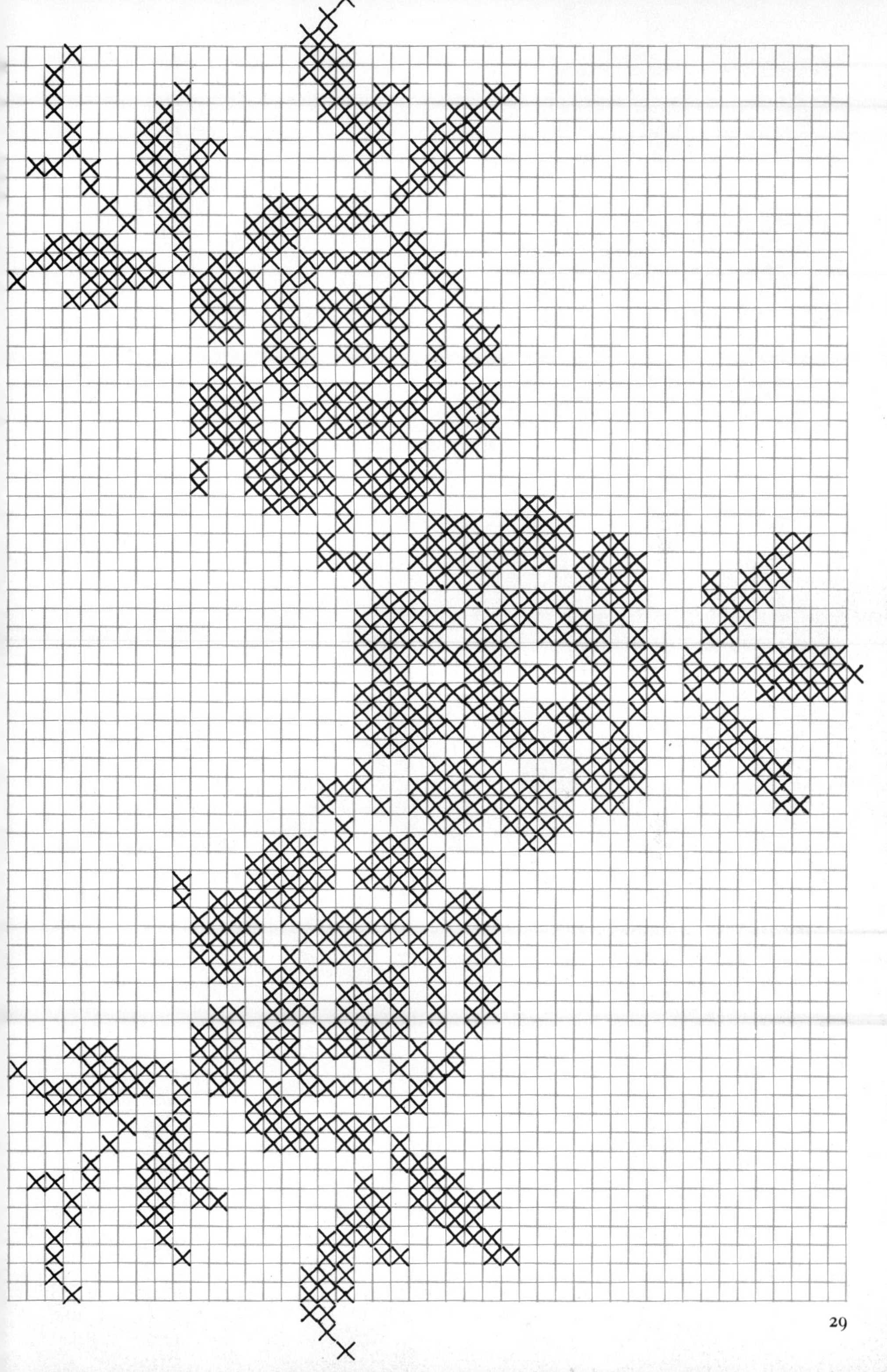

Tree motif in black, sewn on a rough cotton fabric.

Flower barrow on the back pocket of white jeans. The barrow is one colour, the flowers in many different colours.

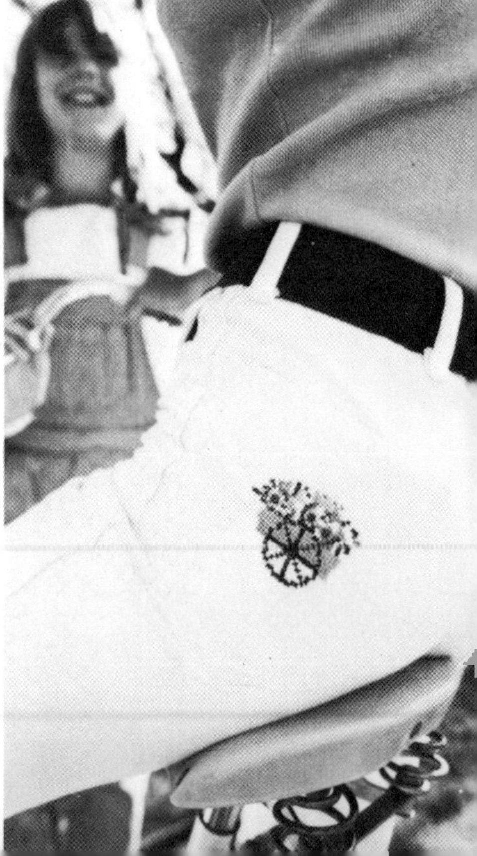

IP

K·L

LISEN

1977

ANNA

KL

ELSA
JONASON

K L

Cross-stitch on a towelling robe. Use three strands of embroidery thread, or crochet thread.

A cockerel in black and light blue on a white shirt. A triangle is sewn at the top of the side opening.

Baskets with flowers in different reds embroidered on white shirts. There is also a fly on the shirt on the left! See p. 61 for the pattern.

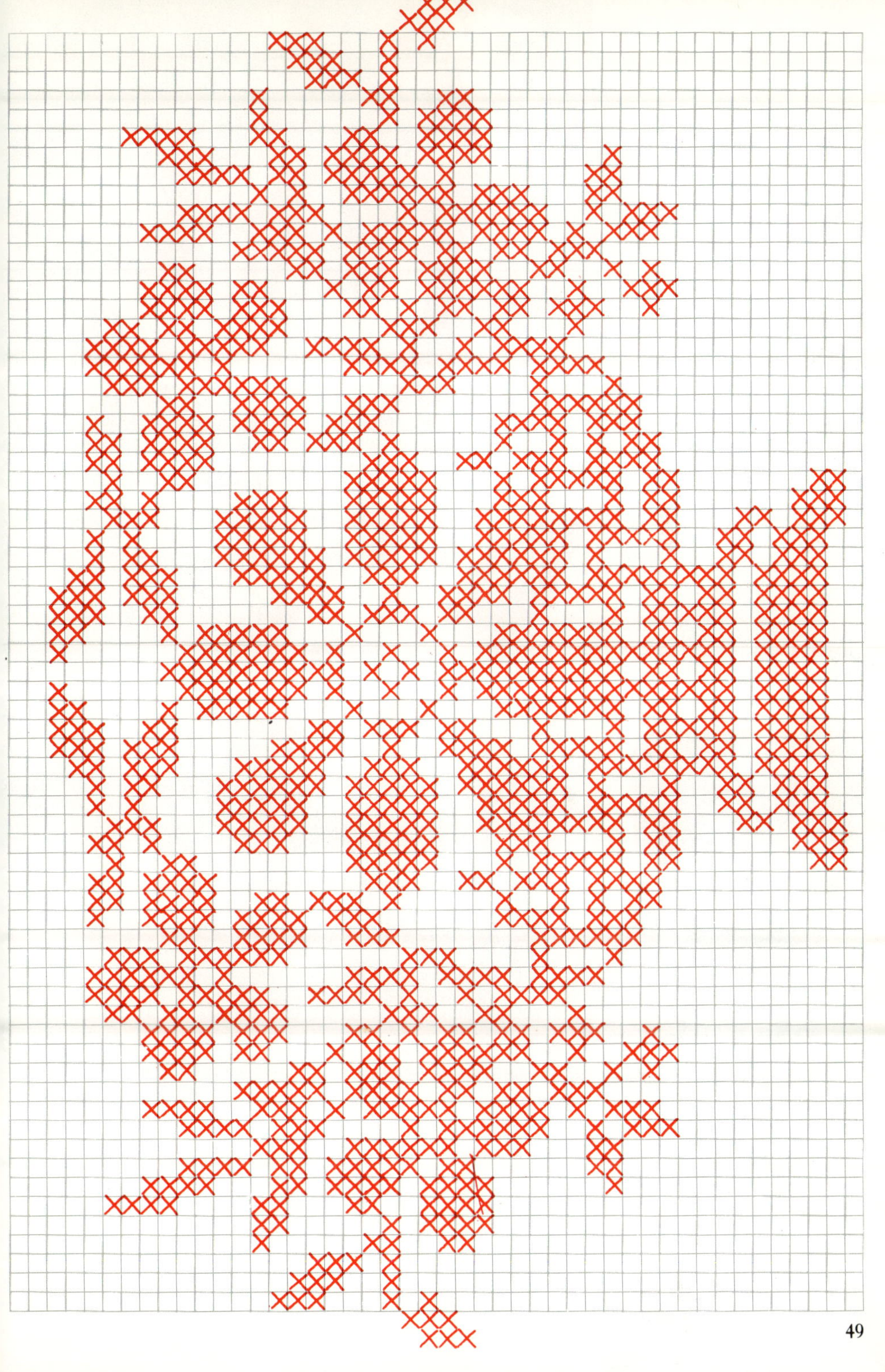

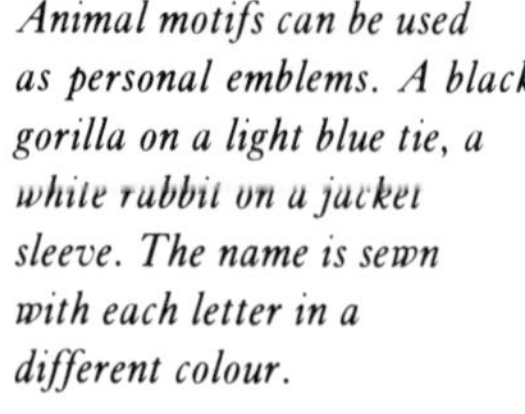

Animal motifs can be used as personal emblems. A black gorilla on a light blue tie, a white rabbit on a jacket sleeve. The name is sewn with each letter in a different colour.

A big rabbit in white cross-stitch on a skirt. This is sewn directly on to the fabric following the square print.

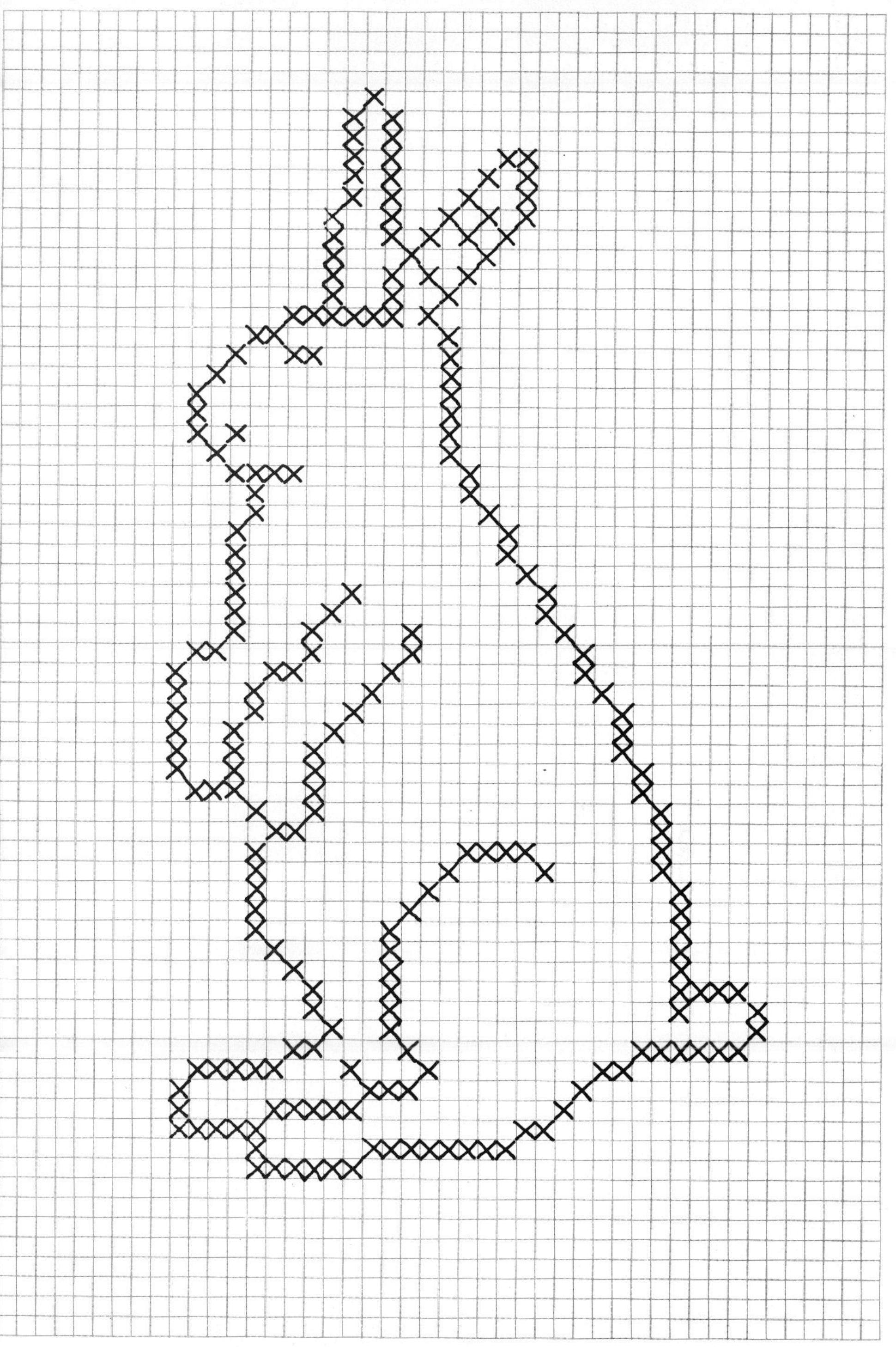

On the front of the jacket swims a swan: on the back a moon, stars, initials and the year.

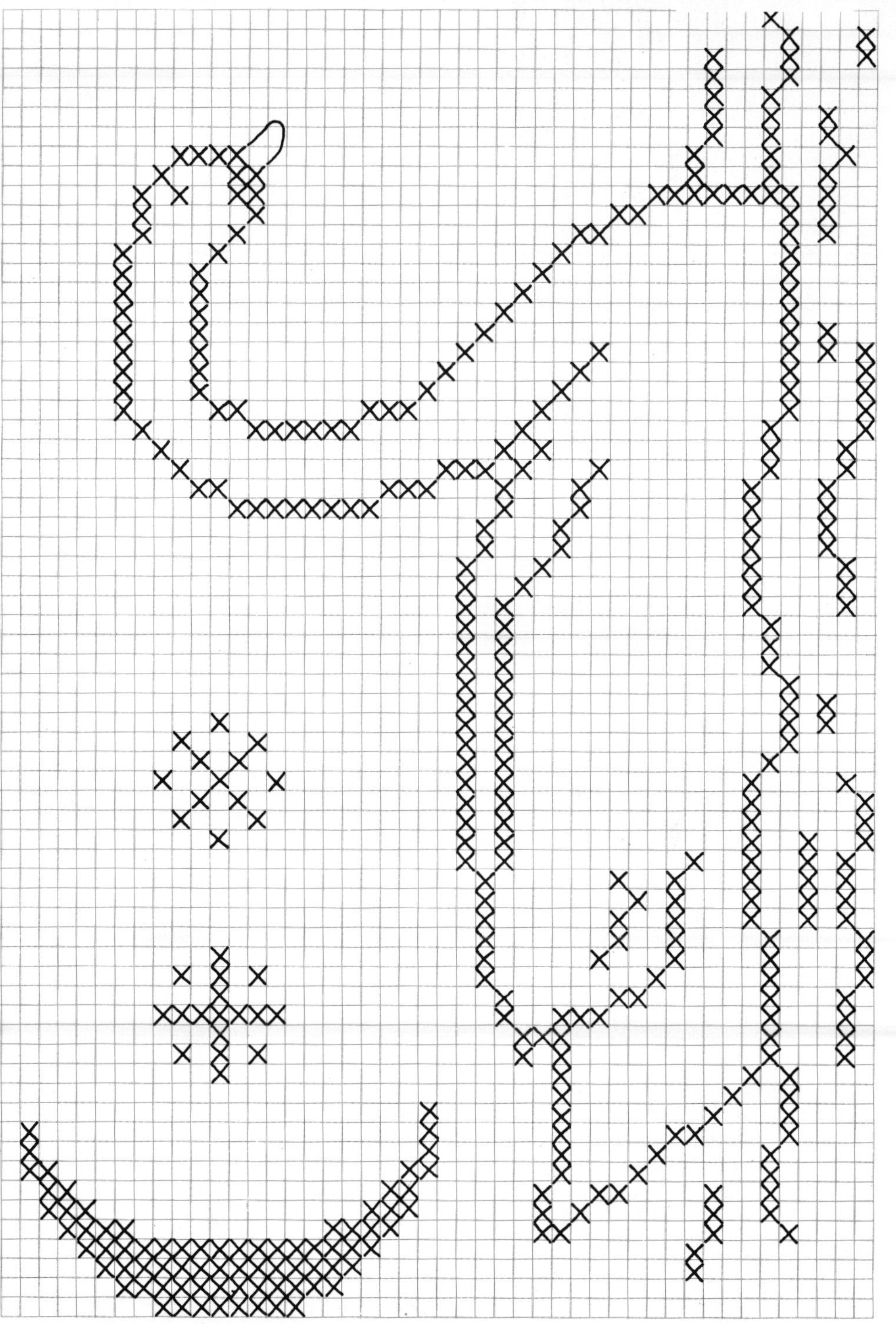

1977

(*The rest of this pattern comes on p. 90.*)

centre ↑

Lucia's shirt has a row of tiny red hearts and squares. You will find the heart-shaped pattern on p. 45.

An apron with a pretzel and a teacup. The pattern for the cup is on p. 76.

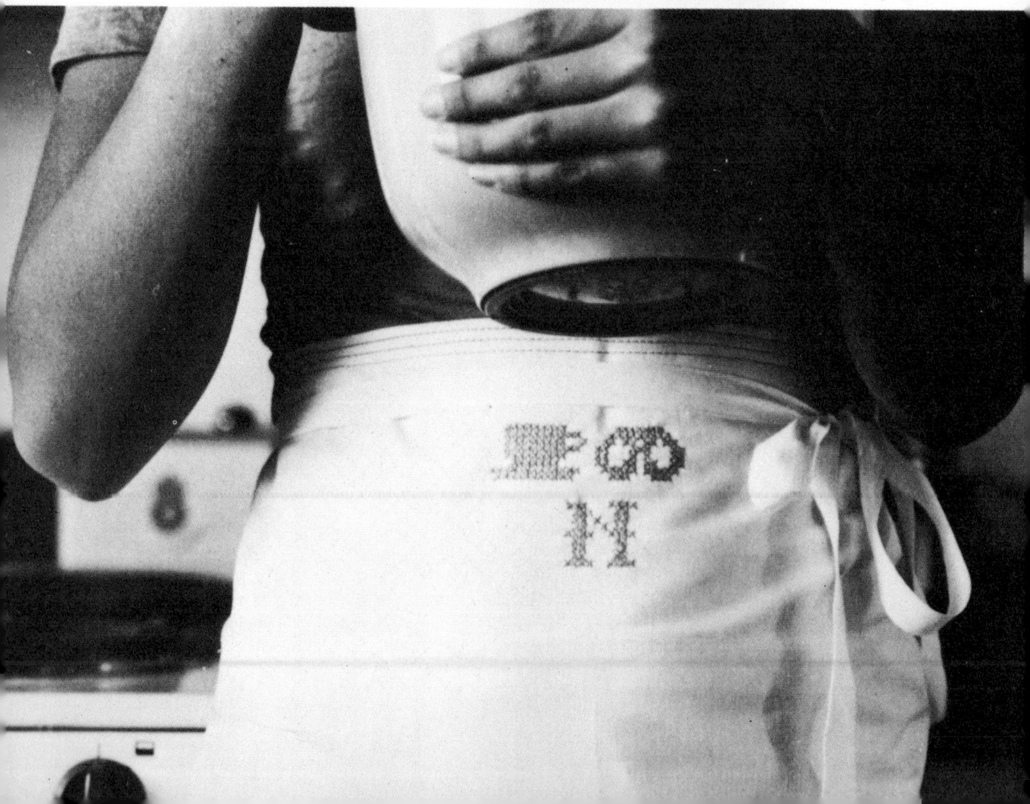

Flies sewn on a pair of espadrilles. The same fly in black and grey on a grand-dad shirt.

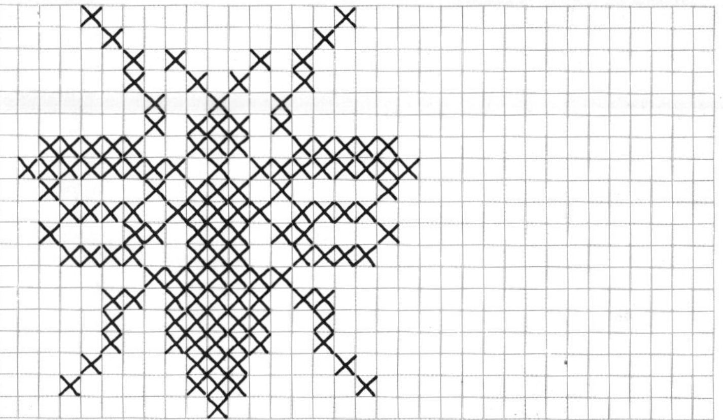

A framed monogram can be very attractive. Sew the frame first so that the letters come in the centre.

A man's shirt worn as a maternity shirt and decorated with cross-stitching.

A flowery chain on the pocket of two blouses. If you want a larger design you can use the pattern with roses shown opposite.

The rest of the rose pattern is on p. 91.)

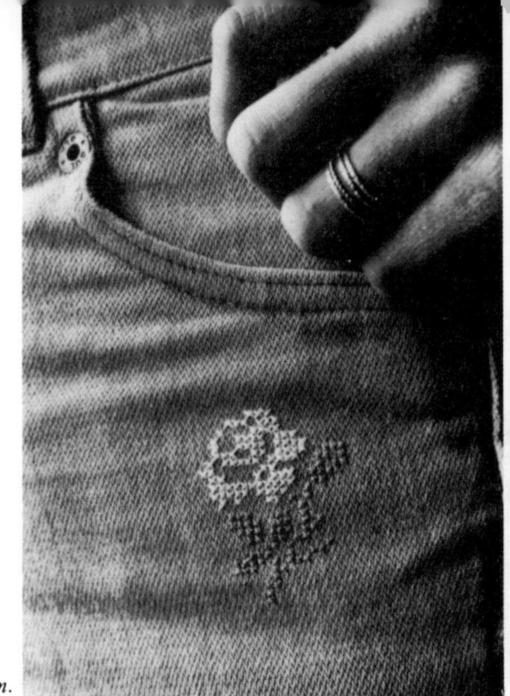

Cross-stitched roses on denim.

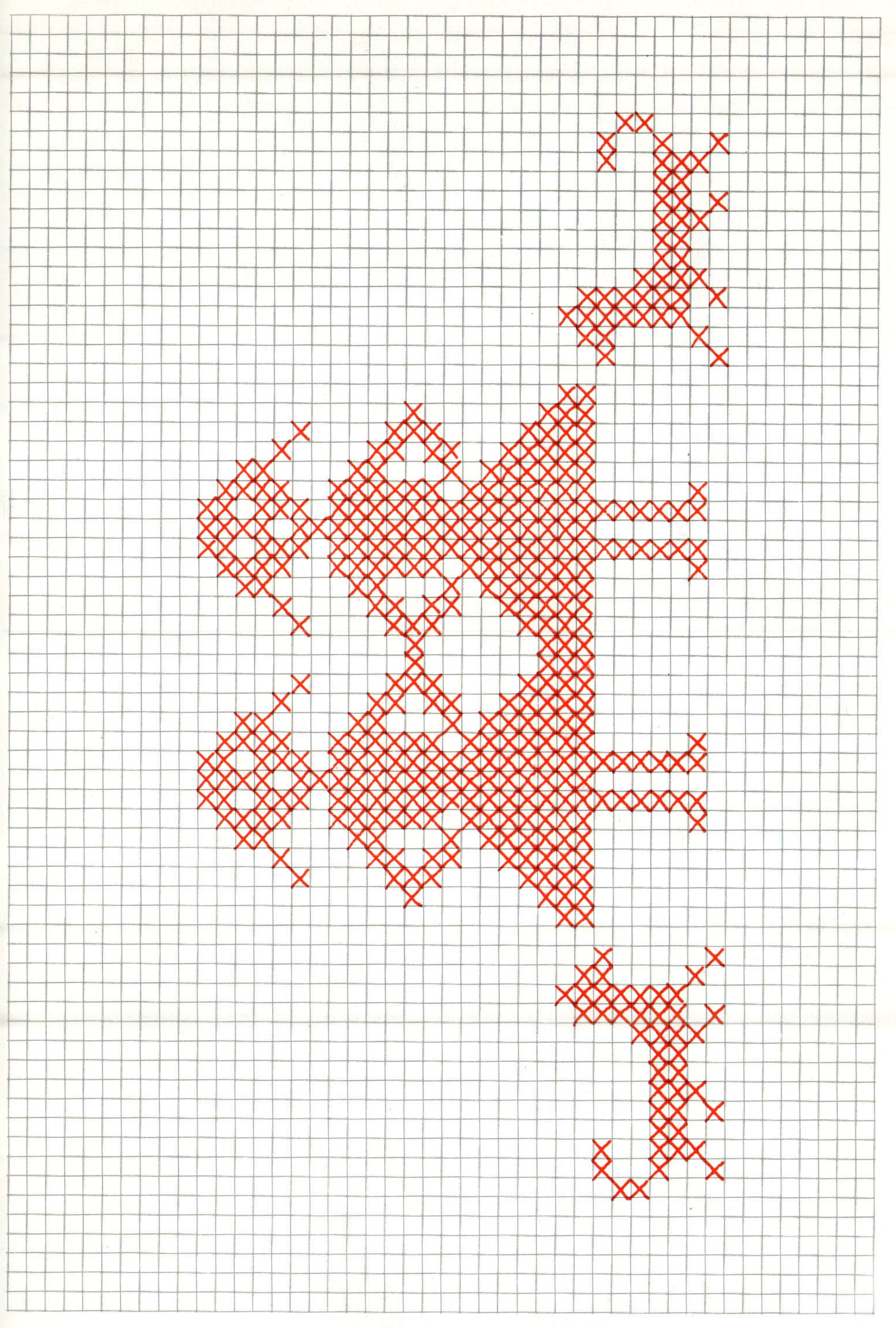

Borders can be sewn on any part of a garment, for example on the buttonhole strip or on the cuffs. The heart-shaped pattern is on p. 45.

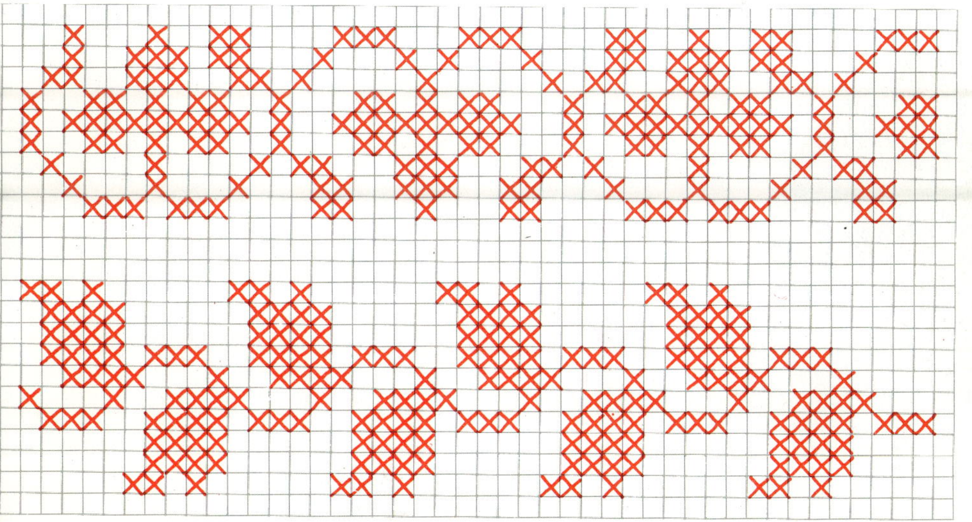

Artist's smock with a single carnation and the year.

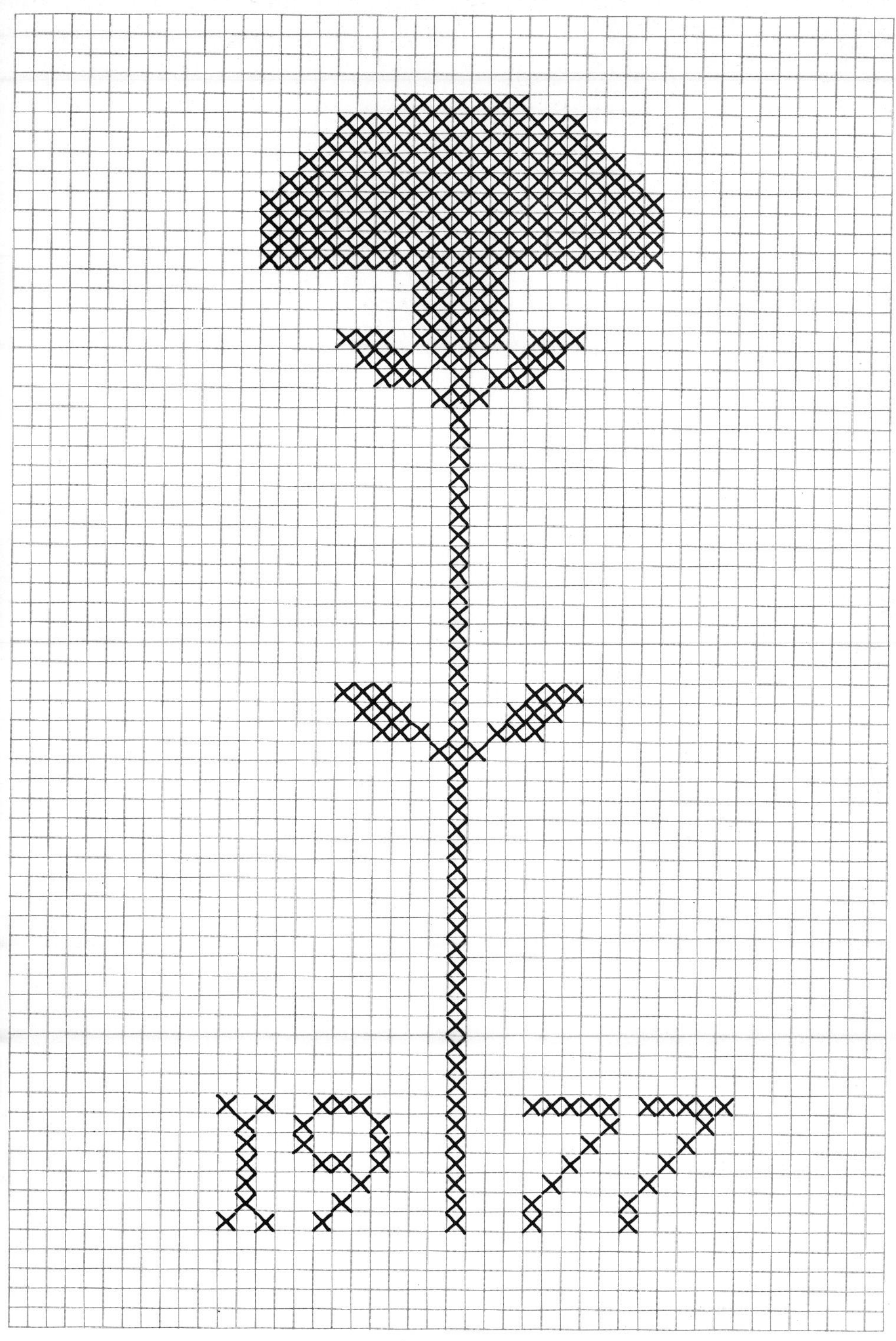
1977

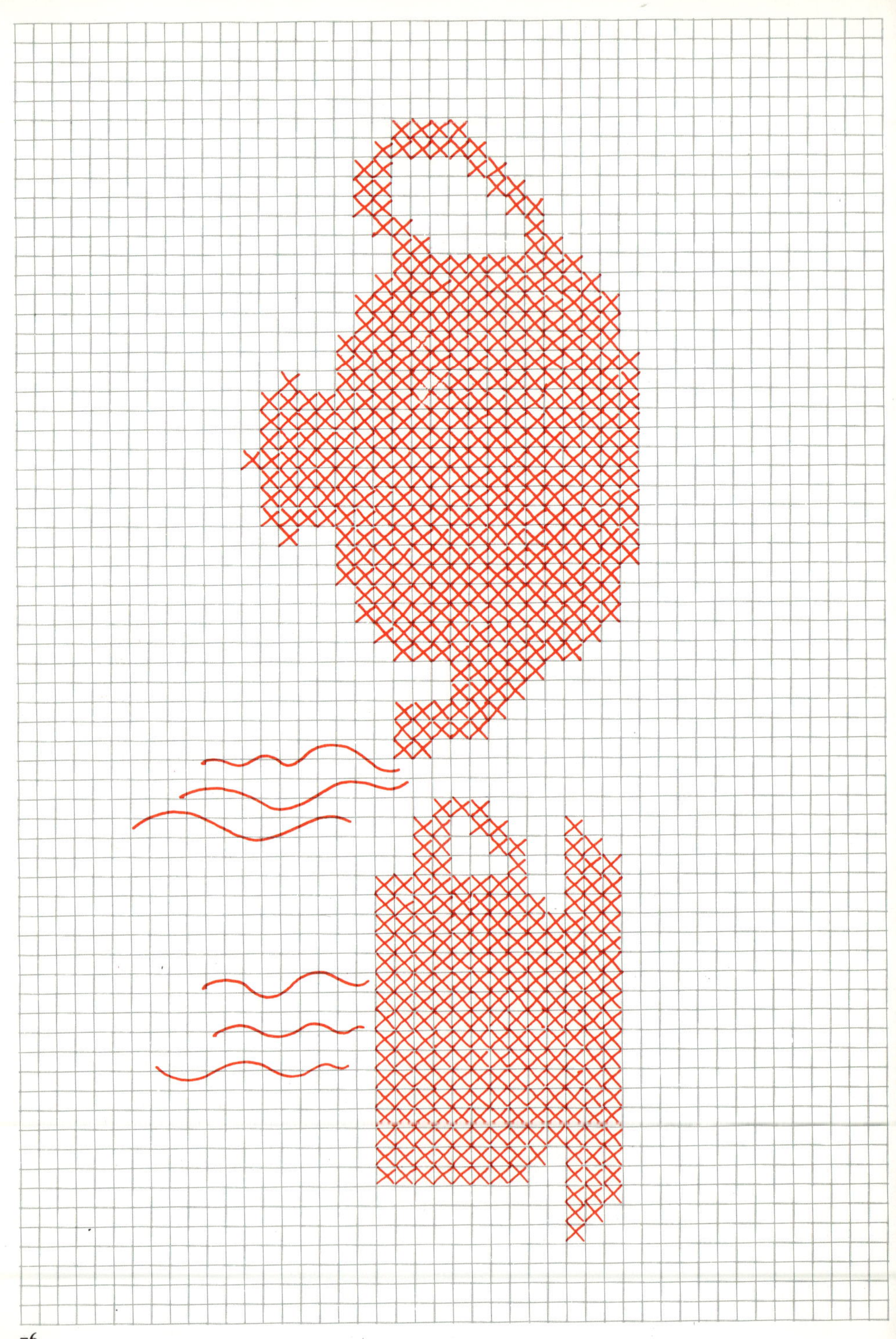

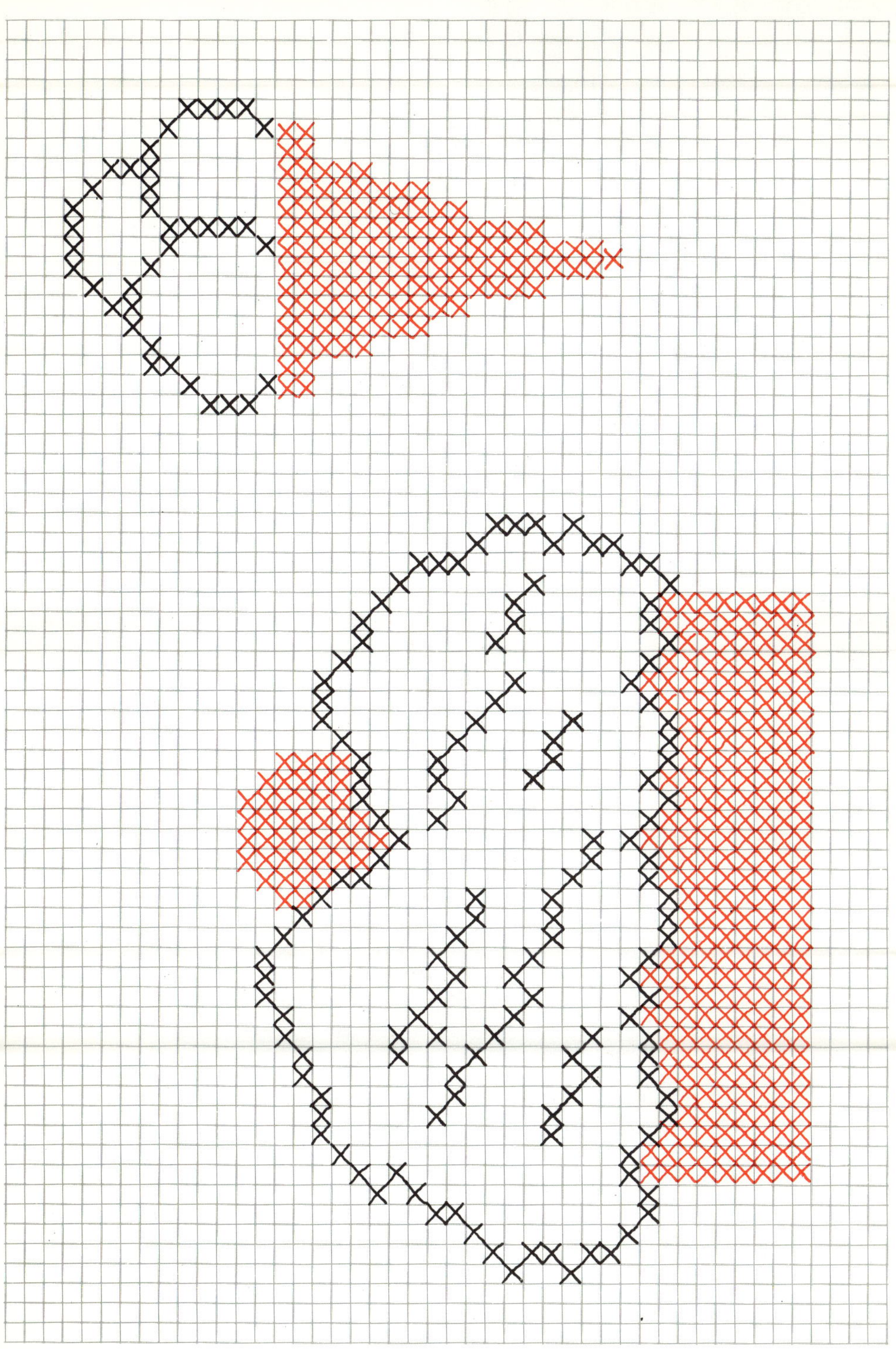

Letters can be combined with small motifs. The pattern for the crown is on p. 17; the dog is on p. 51.

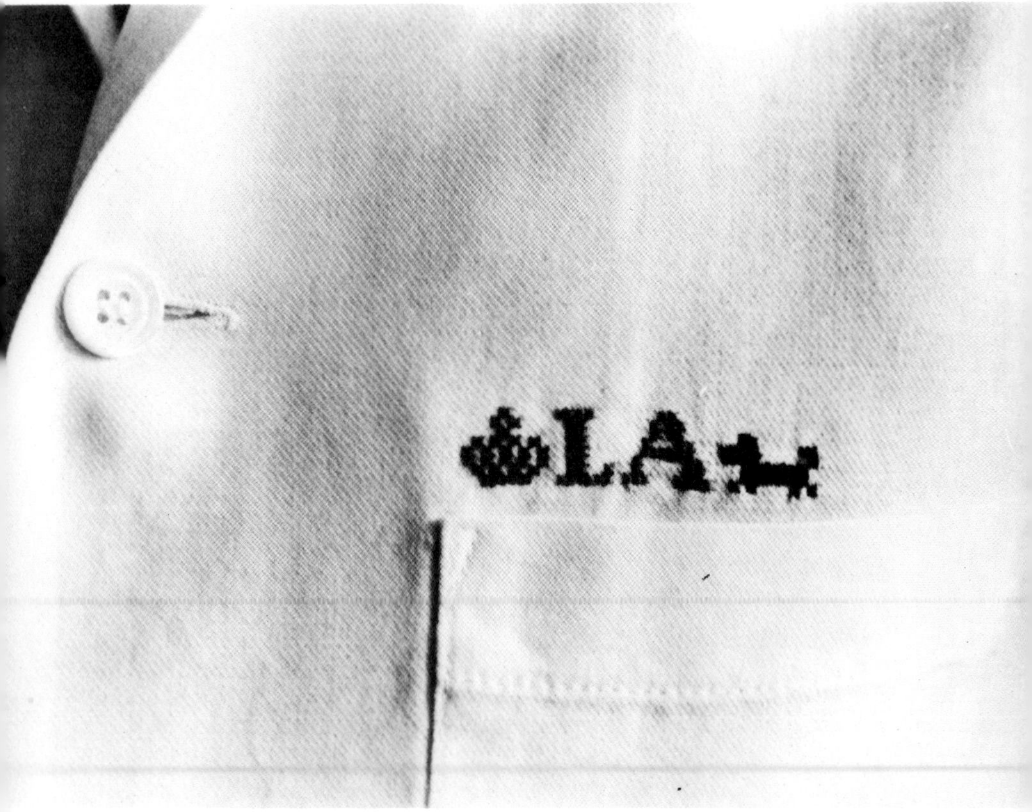

15
14
15
12

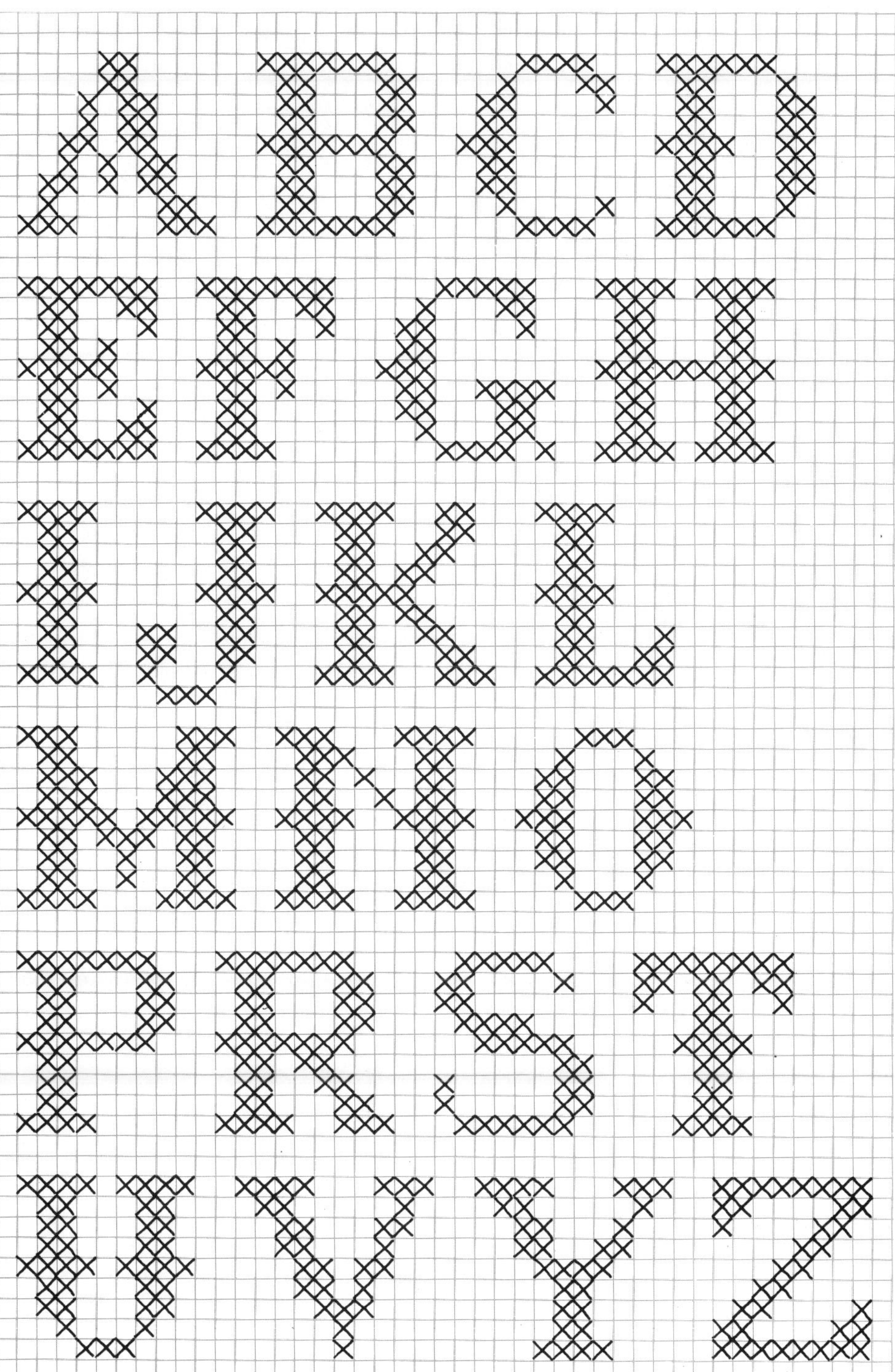

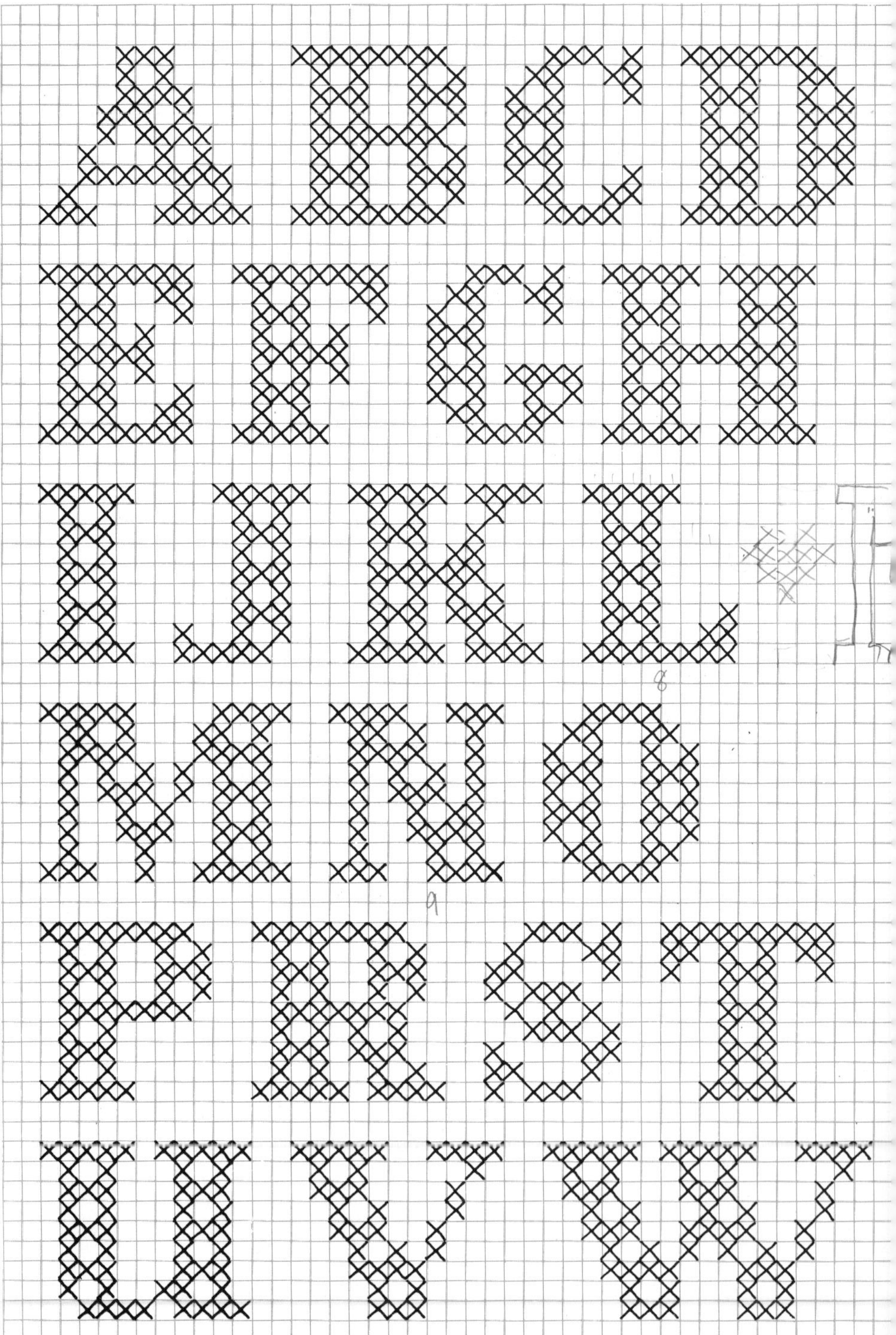

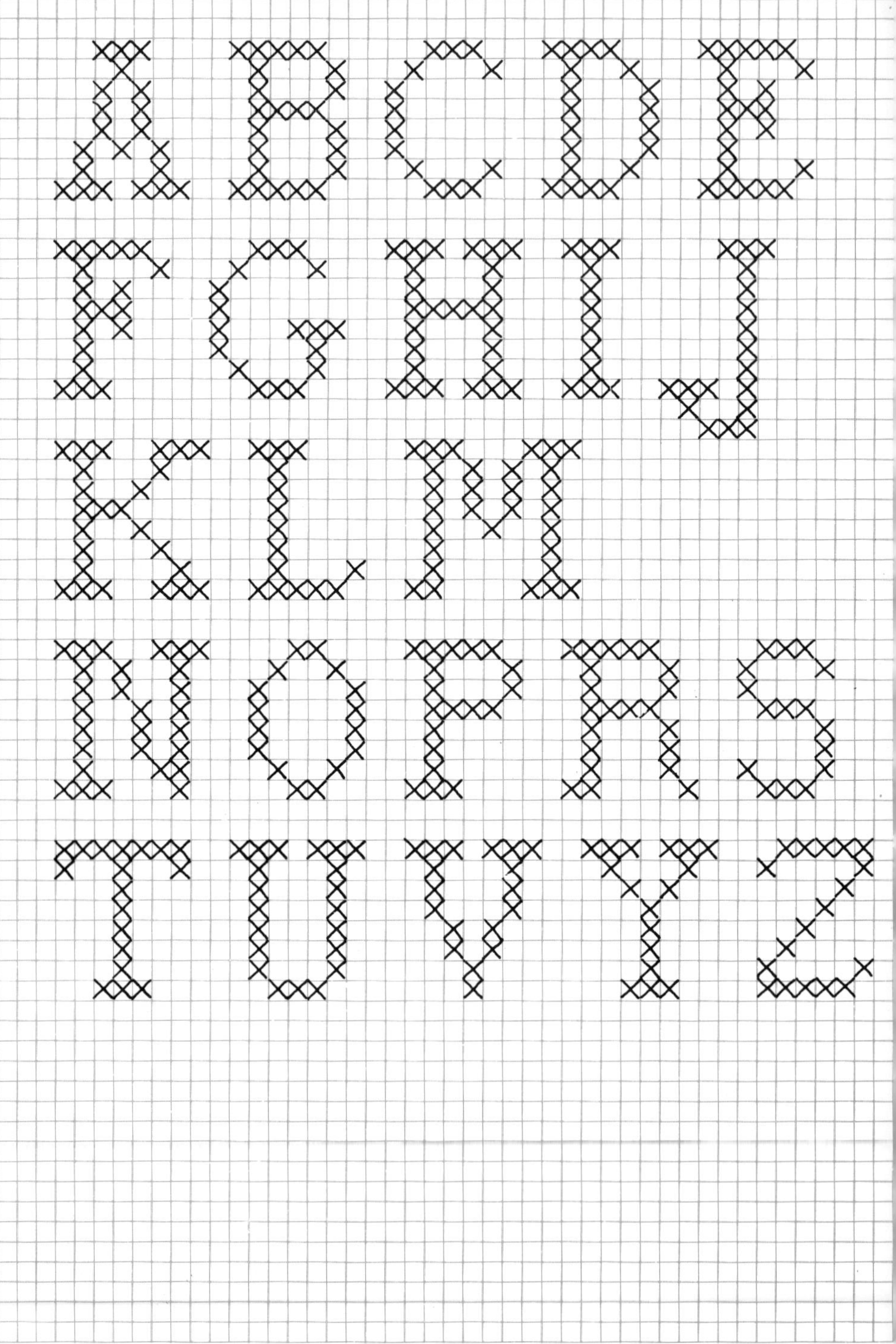

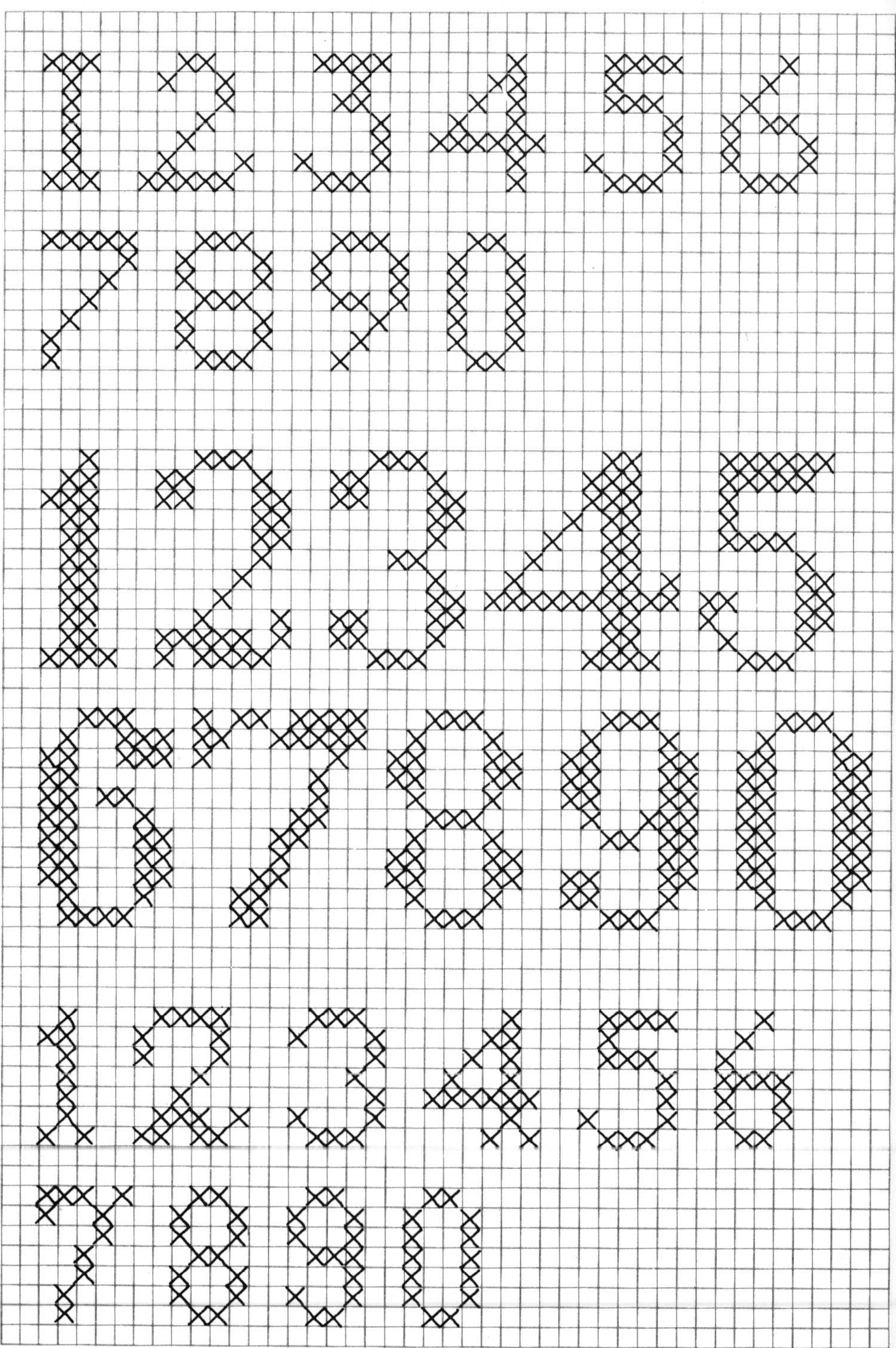

centre ↑

centre ↑

centre

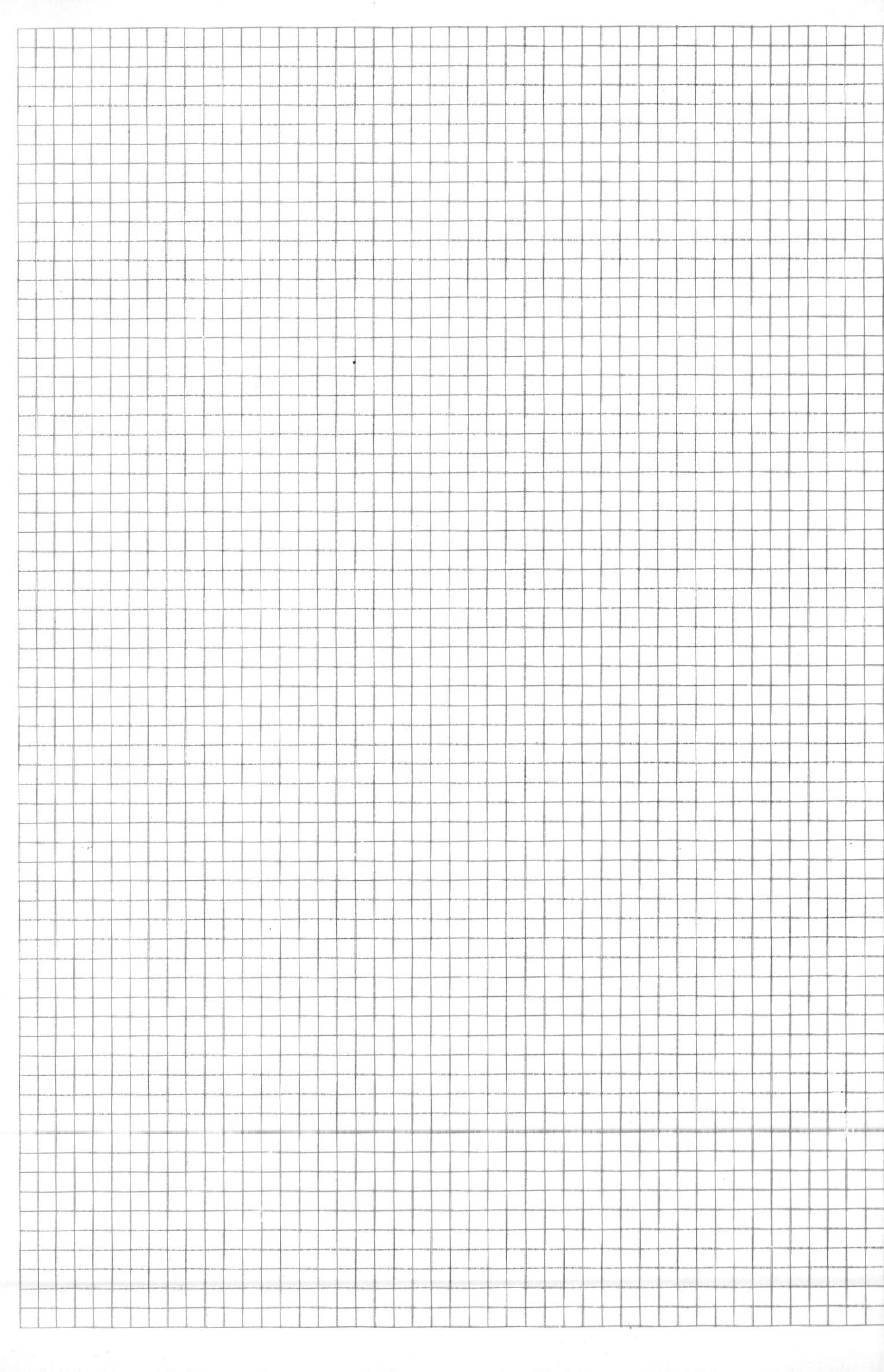